My Favorite Bright Line Recipes

JENNA CARRON

© 2017 by Inciti Publishing, Inc. All rights reserved.

No part of this book may be reproduced in any written, electronic, recording, or photocopying without written permission of the publisher or author. The exception would be in the case of brief quotations embodied in critical articles or reviews and pages where permission is specifically granted by the publisher or author.

Although every precaution has been taken to verify the accuracy of the information contained herein, the author and publisher assume no responsibility for any errors or omissions. No liability is assumed for damages that may result from the use of information contained within.

Cover Design: eCoverLab / Inciti Publishing, Inc.
Interior Design: Scribble
Publisher: Inciti Publishing, Inc.
ISBN: 9781549550874

DEDICATION

Thank you to everyone – doctors, nurses, dieticians, and countless regular folks on the internet – who have helped me over the years to find recipes that suit whatever eating program I was on at the time. You saved my sanity as well as my health.

An extra special thank you to my beloved husband, who cheerfully ate whatever I put in front of him, regardless of how weird, even though he didn't need to be on a special diet. The recipes in this book are the ones for which he declared, "I wouldn't mind eating that every week."

CONTENTS

TITLE PAGE	i
DEDICATION	iii
CONTENTS	v
ACKNOWLEDGMENTS	1
CHAPTER #1: My Story	3
CHAPTER #2: Your Pantry	8
CHAPTER #3: Making It Work	11
CHAPTER #4: Breakfasts	13
CHAPTER #5: Lunches	19
CHAPTER #6: Dinners	25
CHAPTER #7: Salads	38
CHAPTER #8: Sample Meal Plans	41
CHAPTER #9: Final Thoughts	44

ACKNOWLEDGMENTS

First and foremost, I acknowledge the groundbreaking work done in food addiction and long-term healthy eating strategies by Susan Peirce Thompson, PhD. She created Bright Line Eating, and the Bright Line Eating trademark is owned by Bright Line Eating Solutions, LLC. To completely understand the Bright Line Eating methodology, read her book and/or enroll in one of her classes.

Next, thank you to my team of eager cooks who read this book, tried the recipes, and gave me comments to improve it:

Kate Casper
Jonathan Kolber
Arlisa Lewis
Shawna Morris

MY STORY
Chapter One

I have spent most of my adult life battling with diabetes. It started in my mid-twenties. Until then, I'd been a reasonably healthy person – growing up, my father had been a health nut before it was popular, eliminating my beloved hot dogs and bacon because of carcinogens, limiting eggs to twice a week, and special ordering wheat bran from someplace in Europe to add to his Shredded Wheat. (Since he also added blueberries, the resulting purple gruel was completely revolting to look at. Fortunately he was okay with my eating Cheerios instead, as long as I didn't add sugar.) I was a regular at the gym, had achieved my green belt in Tae Kwon Do, and was half way to achieving my blue.

Then, I suddenly started gaining weight. I gained 20 pounds in a single year. My cholesterol, which had always been 174 – 176 (my dad had us tested for the first time when I was twelve) jumped up to 199. When I had it tested again, it had risen to 211. Something was clearly wrong.

The doctors I went to all shook their heads, told me I was obese, and that if I just lost the weight, that would fix everything else.

I knew that wasn't the right answer. I hadn't changed what I was eating or how much I was exercising. There was something wrong with me that was causing the weight gain, not the other way around.

Desperate for an answer, I discovered Dr. Mark Hyman, an early supporter of food sensitivities. Unlike food allergies, which are obvious because they cause hives, dramatic swelling, or vomiting, food sensitivities are like the drops of water that slowly erode a mountain.

I visited his clinic in Massachusetts, and had thorough testing done. They took 13 vials of blood. They tested my blood sugar after overnight fasting, then again after I drank a vile potion of grape flavored liquid sugar. The bad news was that I had Metabolic Syndrome, a pre-diabetic condition where multiple systems in the body begin failing. The good news was that the cause was clear. I had food sensitivities. Oh, boy, did I have food sensitivities! My food was literally poisoning me.

He put me on an elimination diet. Which, if you've never tried it, basically removes all foods that you have any interest whatsoever in eating, leaving you with the most boring foods imaginable. You can't even eat things like tomatoes or potatoes. And do you have any idea how many sauces and condiments contain vinegar? Pretty much all of them.

My life revolved around food. I had to make everything from scratch, could not eat out, and could not use any convenience foods. I had to make at least two trips a week to the grocery store to buy produce at the peak of freshness. I hunted down obscure health foods that didn't contain any of the forbidden ingredients.

It worked. My cholesterol dropped to 153, the weight came off, and the persistent sinus headaches that had plagued me on and off since my teens disappeared completely. I was such a success story that he used my case study as "Patient C" when he presented his findings at a major medical conference ... just before he became a household name with multiple best-selling books and appearances on Oprah.

So if his diet program worked, what was the problem? The problem was that I couldn't eat the way he recommended and still have time to do anything else. I would wake up, cook breakfast, make a brown bag lunch, go to work, work a full day plus overtime, come home, cook dinner, eat dinner, read for an hour or so, then collapse into bed to do it all over the next day. I stuck it out for the 9 months necessary to give the program a fair try, but I was literally counting the days until "freedom" at the end.

I made a few long-lasting changes to my diet. I went from consuming milk at every meal, to limiting my dairy intake. I stopped eating bread at every meal.

But I wanted to eat out with my friends. The crew from work would go to local restaurants at lunch, and my best friend and I would often have dinner at the mall followed by shopping or a movie.

I wanted my time back. So I stopped making everything from scratch (and I do mean everything—Dr. Hyman's regime even called for making your own soup stock) and started buying convenience foods.

Whenever the symptoms became too great to ignore – debilitating sinus headaches, swelling in my feet and legs that made my ankle bones disappear, or hives all over my forearms – I would dutifully remove the allergens from my diet for a few days, until I felt better. Then gradually, they would return.

Meanwhile, I tried other diet programs, hoping to get rid of the weight that had also returned. I had good luck initially with the Atkins diet, until I was diagnosed with cancer. I could either focus on what I was eating, or on my treatment. I focused on the treatment, and stocked my pantry with comfort foods. My post-operative depression was so severe that I literally stopped eating, as I simply could not summon the mental energy to decide what to cook. Sometimes I'd empty a bag of tortilla chips onto a plate, melt a block of cheese over the top, fill a bowl with salsa, and declare that was dinner. That was on a good night.

Fast forward. After watching the documentary *Forks Over Knives*, my husband and I immediately decided that we should try becoming vegans. The following week, I had a routine doctor's appointment, where my doctor informed me that my Metabolic Syndrome had finally crossed the line into full-fledged Type II Diabetes. More importantly, my liver was failing. It was only working at about 1/3 efficiency. I explained that we'd just made the decision to go vegan, and he suggested we see what effect that had on my numbers before trying any medicine.

We managed to stay vegan for about 9 months, which was long enough to allow my liver to repair itself. We managed to stay vegetarian for over a year. But eventually, the same problems that derailed my previous dietary changes derailed me again. I wanted a life, which included comfort foods, eating out with friends, and convenience so that I wasn't always at the grocery store or farmers' market.

Then I read *Bright Line Eating*. Suddenly, so many things became clear! Why was I more likely to fail at dinner time after successfully eating according to my diet plan for breakfast and lunch? Why would breaking my diet at all lead to binge eating of forbidden food? Why did I never seem to successfully navigate the tightrope of life and food for more than a few months at a time?

Bright Line Eating gave me a workable plan. A strict guideline for how many foods of each category – protein, starch, fruit, vegetable, and fat – to consume each day, as well as when during the day to consume them. But more importantly, four simple rules that, even if I did everything else wrong, would keep me on the plan.

I immediately jumped on to Amazon, looking for the companion cookbook. There wasn't one. There were cookbooks using Bright Line Eating in the title, but reviews indicated they were cheap attempts to cash in on a popular trend, and didn't even stick to the diet. I had to cull through all of my many cookbooks, from all of the previous eating programs, to find recipes that would work in the new paradigm.

Unlike all of my previous dietary experiments, it was easy. After dinner each night, well-fed and relaxed while my husband did the dishes, I would plan out the next day's meals. When tomorrow arrived, I would cook and eat the meals I'd planned out. In the first month, I effortlessly lost 20 pounds. The weight continued to come off, a few pounds each month, with no cravings, no obsessing over forbidden foods, and no impact to my lifestyle. We continued going to weekly pot lucks with friends, and I had absolutely no desire to eat the sugary, starchy "treats".

I felt good. I looked good. But what was going on inside? Was it working? As a diabetic, I have to have my blood tested every 6 months. The most important measurement is the A1C level, a measure of your average blood sugar levels over the past 3 months. 6.0% is the threshold for a diabetes diagnosis. 7.0% is the threshold for no longer managing with diet and exercise, and requiring medication.

In all of the years since I'd been diagnosed with Type II Diabetes, my A1C level had never been lower than 6.1% or higher than 6.6%. My first blood test after being on the program for just 2 months was 5.9%. That was a pre-diabetic level! And it continued to fall.

My uncle was diagnosed with diabetes. I typed up a bunch of recipes and mailed them to him. Then my brother was diagnosed with diabetes. I shared my recipes with him.

Which brings me to today, and this book. For anyone who has read *Bright Line Eating*, and wants a few suggestions about how to start, or for anyone who is looking for a diabetic-friendly set of recipes, here are my favorites that helped turn my health around. I hope they can do the same for you.

YOUR PANTRY

Chapter Two

There are many tips and tricks that you can use to make eating according to the Bright Line guidelines easier and more convenient. Here are my favorite time savers and meal enhancers to keep in the pantry.

Celery. Buy the full bunches, not the celery hearts. Not only are they much cheaper, but you can use the tops and inner leafy stalks to make **Celery Lentil Soup** for a real flavor boost.

Dried lentils or split peas. I am not a fan of brown lentils. I am also not a fan of green split peas. However, I have discovered that I enjoy the taste of red lentils and yellow split peas. Experiment for yourself, and see which varieties you like best. The different colors have similar nutritional profiles but quite unique tastes, so don't judge them all by a bad experience you had with one.

Eggs. Fresh eggs from a local farm or farmers' market are ideal. The next best choice are free-range eggs, where the chickens wandered around the farm eating bugs as well as their grain. Next best are cage-free.

Fish. When the salmon are running, buy fresh-caught salmon. It's well worth the extra money and preparation time for the intense flavor. The rest of the year, frozen salmon fillets make wonderful pre-measured serving sizes. If you're like me and want your fish to have more flavor than standard white fish, try catfish. It's more flavorful than tilapia, and about the same price. My local Target carries fresh catfish in the meat and fish section. If you rarely eat tuna, spring for albacore instead of chunk white. It's much better tasting. I've heard, however, that it contains more mercury because of the part of the fish that it comes from, so if you eat a lot of tuna, get line-caught tuna, which have less overall mercury.

Garlic. Buy minced garlic packed in water and store it in your refrigerator. ½ teaspoon of minced garlic equals one clove of garlic. Never worry about running out of garlic, or having your garlic go moldy, soft, hard, or weirdly gelatinous. Minced garlic is usually available in the fresh produce sections of the supermarket.

Ginger. You may have to hunt for it, but ginger is also sold minced in a jar or as a paste in a tube. If you're lucky, it's with the minced garlic. Sometimes it is with the fresh herbs or in a refrigerated case near the salad greens. Not only do you not need to worry about running out, or about your ginger root going bad, you also don't have to mess around with peeling and grating fresh ginger root.

Lemons. I keep fresh lemons on the counter in my fruit basket, since I drink lemon water every morning. I have a dedicated cutting board for the lemon, and store my partially cut lemon cut-side down on the board, next to the electric kettle. That makes it super easy to make **Lemon Water** in the morning, when I may or may not be awake.

Lemon juice. Food purists claim that nothing beats the juice of a fresh lemon. I think the convenience of pre-squeezed lemon juice more than outweighs any slight improvement in taste. If taste really matters to you, spring for the Volcano brand lemon juice, imported from Italy, sold in Costco.

Oatmeal. If you think oatmeal comes in flakes in a canister, and turns into a gluey soup with the taste and texture of wall paper paste when boiled, you're in for a delightful surprise. Steel cut oatmeal has a wonderful, nutty flavor, and is now available in quick-cooking varieties. My favorite is Bob's Red Mill, which we now special order in 7 pound bags. Part of that is because my husband eats a quarter of a pound of oatmeal for breakfast, compared to my one-ounce Bright Line serving size.

Orange and lemon zest. Sure, you can zest your fruit as part of a recipe. But what if you're making something that calls for zest without using any of the corresponding fruit? Dried orange and lemon zest to the rescue. They can be found in the spice aisle of your supermarket.

Salt. I am fond of Himalayan pink salt, since it contains over 180 trace minerals. Modern foods grown in industrial farms have very few trace minerals left in them, and I have to think that our bodies do better with a larger palette of basic building blocks to choose from. If you cannot get the pink salt (available in both bulk and table top grinders from Costco), you can still get a variety of trace elements from sea salt, although unlike pink salt and iodized table salt, sea salt is low in iodine.

Soup stock. My go-to soup stock was a dry powder that could be mixed with water, and did not need to be used within 5 days of opening, unlike premade soup stocks. Unfortunately, it contains sugar as its second ingredient, which makes it off-limits. The Knorr brand of bouillon cubes list sugar as the fifth ingredient, which makes it acceptable for emergency use. My primary soup stocks now are boxed chicken and vegetable stocks with no sugar. The chicken stock is available by the case at Costco, and I was able to find both sugar-free chicken and vegetable stocks at my local Target. (Fair warning: my local Target has an amazing organic produce and health foods section, in keeping with what sells here. The Target by my parents sells none of the healthy foods I consider staples.)

Tomatoes. I use a mix of heritage grape and cherry tomatoes, available at both Costco and my local Target. These are perfect for adding to my nightly salad or my luncheon vegetables, and come in an appealing mix of colors to add visual interest. You can always keep a few cans of organic diced tomatoes (available by the case at Costco, or individually at your local supermarket) on hand for when you need a lot of tomatoes.

MAKING IT WORK
Chapter Three

Since these are my favorite recipes, and I only have to cook for my husband and myself, the recipes are obviously geared toward ones that work for one or two people, and the portion sizes are based on the female portion sizes.

If you are a man, in general you will increase your serving size for protein by half again. So if a serving size is 4 ounces of cooked meat, your serving size will be 6 ounces of cooked meat. The exceptions are beans (6 ounce serving size for everyone) and milk/yogurt (8 ounce serving size for everyone).

If you're cooking for a family, double or triple the recipe size to feed the correct number of people. You may need to experiment a bit to get the right amount of sauce to accompany each recipe, since there is usually extra.

I also give approximate weights in many of the two-person recipes. I do measure my portion by weight. I just serve my husband the remainder. It's approximately one serving size, and much easier for me.

Similarly, onions are usually given by volume, not weight. That's because they're not counting toward the vegetable allowance. As long as there is less than 2 tablespoons of them in each serving, I consider them to fall under the seasonings/condiments rule. If you don't agree with this interpretation, feel free to modify the total vegetable weight of recipes to include the weight of the onions.

You may notice that recipes are rarely complete combinations of all of the food groups you should be eating for a specific meal. Mix and match recipes, then supplement with fruit, vegetables, and fats as needed.

Fruit is simple to add – keep a basket of apples and oranges on the counter, as well as fresh and frozen berries in the fridge and freezer. In season, you can add kiwis and pomegranates. To serve a kiwi, slice it in half in the narrow direction, and slide a soup spoon between the flesh and the skin to pop the skin off. To serve a pomegranate, cut the skin into quarters and submerge in a large bowl filled with water. Break the pomegranate into quarters. For each quarter, holding the skin firmly, press with your fingers into the center of the quarter, forcing the fruit inside-out. Strip out the arils (the bright red things containing the seeds) with your thumbs, and discard the remaining rind. The arils will float to the top of the bowl. Discard any that are strangely colored (white ones are not yet ripe, and gray or brown ones have started to rot), as well as any remaining pieces of pith that sink to the bottom.

My favorite choice for an added fat serving is 25 pistachios. This takes the place of chips or fries at lunch, providing the same slow-eating, salty crunch. You can also add 2 ounces of avocado to your lunch, and a tablespoon of butter (or Earth Balance buttery spread for the dairy-averse) or olive oil to your vegetables at dinner.

BREAKFASTS
Chapter Four

B reakfast is the most important meal of the day, according to most diet wisdom. It lets your body know that food is available, so it's okay to be active and alert instead of taking a long nap to conserve calories.

It's also a great way to have a quick fix of satisfaction and confidence that another day has been met with you keeping to your eating plan.

My favorite breakfasts include lemon water instead of tea or coffee – it's good for the liver, and now that I'm eating healthily, I don't need the caffeine to get started in the morning. I also have a few favorite oatmeal dishes – feel free to make them with other acceptable grains if you're not an oatmeal fan – and a variety of egg dishes for my protein. Not included in this cookbook but often eaten are fried, scrambled, over-easy, soft-boiled, and poached eggs. If I had a late dinner the night before and do not expect to be very hungry, I'll have a light protein of 4 ounces of cottage cheese with a sprinkle of paprika on it, or 2 ounces of cheese.

Lemon Water

Serves: 1
Exchanges: None

> 1 lemon
> 2 Tbsp unflavored Colloidal Minerals (optional)
> 8 oz water

1) Boil water.
2) Cut off and discard the end of the lemon, so that the inner flesh is exposed. Slice three thin slices from the lemon. (Store the remainder of the lemon cut-side down, to prevent it from drying out.)
3) Place lemon slices in the bottom of a coffee cup. Pour Colloidal Minerals (if using) over the lemon slices. Add the boiling water.

Colloidal Minerals (Fulvic Acid Trace Minerals) are available from NOW in both unflavored and flavored varieties. You can find bottles at health food or vitamin stores, or order them online. The flavored variety contains a sweetener, so be sure you get the unflavored variety. Since it contains citric acid, it has a slight lemony flavor, making this an excellent combination. The trace minerals include boron, calcium, chromium, copper, iron, magnesium, manganese, molybdenum, phosphorus, potassium, selenium, silver, sodium, sulfur, and zinc.

Oatmeal and Banana
Serves: 1
Exchanges: 1 grain, 1 fruit

> 1 oz fast cooking steel cut oatmeal
> ¼ teaspoon salt (or to taste)
> ½ cup water
> 1 banana

1. In a microwave safe bowl, put the oatmeal and salt.
2. Add water and stir.
3. Microwave for 2 minutes on high. Stir. Microwave for another 2 minutes on high. Stir. Remove from microwave.
   Caution: Bowl will be very hot!
4. Meanwhile, peel and slice the banana. Add banana slices to oatmeal.

I recommend Bob's Red Mill Quick Cooking Steel Cut Oats. According to the packaging, this brand won the coveted Golden Spurtle award for the best tasting oatmeal. (A spurtle is a traditional oatmeal stirring utensil.) Having tasted a wide variety of different oatmeals over the years, I can understand why.

Berry Good Oatmeal

Serves: 1
Exchanges: 1 grain, 1 fruit

> 1 oz fast cooking steel cut oatmeal
> ¼ teaspoon salt (or to taste)
> ½ cup water
> 6 ounces berries, any variety, fresh or frozen

1. In a microwave safe bowl, put the oatmeal and salt.
2. Add water and stir.
3. Microwave for 2 minutes on high. Stir. Microwave for another 2 minutes on high. Stir. Remove from microwave.
   Caution: Bowl will be very hot!
4. Stir berries into oatmeal. Allow oatmeal to sit for 1 minute, then stir again.

Costco sells an excellent antioxidant blend of strawberries, blueberries, blackberries, and pomegranate seeds that works very well in this recipe.

Gruyere Egg
Serves: 1
Exchanges: 1 protein

>1 egg
>1 oz gruyere cheese, shredded
>salt and pepper to taste
>2 teaspoons water

1. Spray a skillet or nonstick frying pan with nonstick cooking spray, or melt a scant amount of coconut oil in the pan. Heat the pan on medium-high.
2. Turn down the heat to medium-low. Crack the egg into the pan. Sprinkle with salt and pepper to taste. Let cook until the bottom of the egg is done, but the top is still soft.
3. Sprinkle the shredded gruyere over the egg. Add water to the pan, cover, and let cook for a few more minutes. The cheese should be melted and the white of the egg should be set.

This dish can be made with any kind of cheese. Mild cheddar or swiss both work well, if they're all you have on hand. However I think nothing beats the combination of mild flavor and smooth meltiness of gruyere.

Rice and Eggs

Serves: 1
Exchanges: 1 protein, 1 grain

> 2 eggs
> 4 oz cooked whole grain rice
> salt and pepper to taste

1. Spray a skillet or nonstick frying pan with nonstick cooking spray, or melt a scant amount of coconut oil in the pan. Heat the pan on medium-high.
2. In a small bowl, beat together the eggs and rice, until all rice grains are thoroughly covered in egg mixture.
3. Turn down the heat to medium-low. Pour the egg mixture into the pan. Sprinkle with salt and pepper to taste. Cook, stirring, until the egg is no longer runny.
4. With a spatula, form the mixture into a pancake shape. Cook until eggs are fully set. Flip once.

This is my favorite breakfast for when I'm not feeling well, and using the modified eating plan of 3 breakfasts per day. It's bland, so it won't upset a queasy tummy, and soft, so it won't irritate a sore throat. If you're not sick, you could spice it up with some dill weed and tarragon, to give it more flavor.

LUNCHES
Chapter Five

Lunches are often the most difficult meal of the day for people on a restricted eating plan. What can you make that morning, or even the night before, that will still taste good hours later? And it needs to be something you can eat without wearing it for the rest of the day, which means no soup for me.

There's a reason that sandwiches are so popular as lunchtime solutions. However, with the rise of healthy eating habits among the general population, you can buy lunch box sets (I got mine at Target) designed to keep all of your salad ingredients separate, so nothing gets soggy or wilted. You can mix the ingredients together right before you eat your lunch.

Egg Salad Boats
Serves: 1
Exchanges: 1 protein, 1 vegetable, 1 oil

> 1 small head of artisanal romaine lettuce
> 2 eggs, hard boiled
> 1 tablespoon mayonnaise
> 1 dash curry powder (or to taste)
> salt and pepper to taste
> paprika for garnish

1. Cut off the bottom of the head of lettuce. Rinse and separate the leaves. Pat dry.
2. Peel the hard boiled eggs and discard the shells. In a medium bowl, crush the eggs.
3. Add mayonnaise, curry powder, salt, and pepper to eggs. Stir until smooth.
4. Assemble the boats. Hold each leaf in one hand so that it makes a bowl shape. Spoon some of the egg mixture into the center of the leaf. Place the filled leaf onto a large plate.
5. If you run out of egg mixture before all of the boats are filled, chop the remaining leaves and serve as a side salad.
6. Sprinkle the filled boats with paprika for a garnish.

If you've never tried curry powder in your egg salad, I highly recommend it. Not only does it make the taste of the eggs really pop, but it gives pale, unappetizing mass produced modern eggs the vibrant yellow gold color of eggs I remember from my childhood and the local chicken farm.

Turkey Salad
Serves: 1
Exchanges: 1 protein, 1 vegetable

>   4 oz deli turkey slices
>   4 oz celery stalks, trimmed
>   2 oz small heritage tomatoes

1. Slice the turkey into bite-sized pieces using your preferred method. (Sometimes I stack all of the slices on top of each other and cut them into cubes, and sometimes I roll the slices up and slice the roll.)
2. Chop the celery. Quarter the tomatoes.
3. Assemble the salad by placing the celery into a bowl, then the tomatoes, and finally the turkey.

This is my go-to lunch. The celery provides a satisfying crunch, the tomatoes give it a hint of sweetness, and I love deli turkey. My favorite is hickory smoked turkey. I could eat it every day, and in fact did eat it almost every day during college – although then I had it as a sandwich on a bagel.

Tuna Salad in a Tomato

Serves: 1
Exchanges: 1 protein, 1 vegetable, 1 oil

>1 large tomato (approximately 6 oz after coring)
>4 oz tuna fish
>1 tablespoon mayonnaise
>1 tablespoon relish or pickle juice (or to taste)

1. Cut the top off of the tomato and core it. If the cored tomato is less than 6 ounces, add small pieces of the top to your scale until you achieve 6 ounces. Turn the tomato upside down over a paper towel or strainer and let it drain.
2. Put the tuna in a small bowl, and break it up with a fork. Add the mayonnaise and either relish or pickle juice. If you have extra bits of tomato on your scale, add them as well. Stir until well combined.
3. Place the tomato, right side up, on a plate. Fill the tomato with the tuna mixture.

Commercial sweet pickle relish does contain sweetener, so check to be sure that the variety you've chosen lists it as the fifth ingredient or lower on the ingredients list. If you're in the early stages of Bright Line Eating and don't want any sugars at all, use the juice from a jar of pickles.

Simple Tuna Nicoise Salad
Serves: 1
Exchanges: 1 protein, 1 vegetable, 1 oil

    6 oz green beans (before trimming)
    1 oz heritage tomatoes (approximately)
    4 oz tuna fish
    1 tablespoon mayonnaise
    1 tablespoon relish or pickle juice (or to taste)

1. Trim the ends off of the green beans, and cut them into inch-long pieces. Weigh them after they've been trimmed – you'll use an appropriate amount of tomatoes to make up a total weight of 6 ounces of vegetables.
2. Put the green beans into a steamer over boiling water. Cover. Steam for 8 minutes.
3. Meanwhile, put the tuna in a small bowl, and break it up with a fork. Add the mayonnaise and either relish or pickle juice. Stir until well combined.
4. Quarter the tomatoes.
5. Drain the green beans and transfer to a plate. Add the tomatoes. Top with tuna mixture.

Traditional Nicoise salad also includes hard boiled eggs and olives. If you're a real purist, decrease the amount of tuna to 3 ounces and add half of a chopped hard-boiled egg, and decrease the total amount of green beans and tomatoes by the weight of your olives.

Burger with Salsa
Serves: 4
Exchanges: 1 protein, 1 vegetable

>1 pound organic ground beef
>¼ cup onion, diced
>¼ cup bell pepper, diced (reserve remainder of bell pepper)
>1 teaspoon Montreal Steak Seasoning
>¼ cup salsa

1. Preheat a gas grill to medium.
2. Divide ground beef into four 4 oz sections.
3. In a bowl, mix each section of ground beef with approximately ¼ of the onions and peppers (some people may prefer more onion, and some may prefer more peppers) until well distributed.
4. Form into 4 patties.
5. Dust tops of patties with seasoning, using more for spicier burgers and less for less spicy burgers.
6. Grill on the gas grill for 8 – 10 minutes, until cooked through but not overcooked.
7. Slice the remaining bell pepper into flat slabs. Weigh out enough bell pepper to make a full 6 oz serving of vegetable, when the diced vegetable and salsa are included. Grill the bell pepper lightly (3 – 5 minutes) on each side.
8. Transfer to four plates. Top with salsa.

This is my famous back-yard barbecue recipe. The onions and pepper in the beef mixture keep it from drying out while cooking, so you can use very lean ground beef. You can also put out mustard and fresh onion slices for people, depending on how they like their hamburgers. If they're not Bright Line Eating, they may also appreciate hamburger buns.

DINNERS
Chapter Six

Dinners for me start with the protein source – is it chicken, fish, or plant-based? My favorite dinners are one-dish meals, where all of the vegetable, protein, and fat exchanges are included in a single serving, although sometimes I'll steam some broccoli or green beans to go on the side.

I also included some options for including an additional grain exchange if you are in maintenance mode of the eating plan, or for your family members if they're not on the same eating plan.

I make a batch of the celery lentil soup every week – usually on the weekends, to finish off the tops and inner leaves of the bunches of celery. In the manner of most soups, it's also a great way to get rid of tomatoes that are starting to get a little wrinkly, carrots that are starting to dry out, or any other not-so-fresh produce left in your refrigerator.

Sweet Mustard Chicken

Serves: 2
Exchanges: 1 protein

>¾ pound of chicken breast
>½ cup chicken broth
>2 tablespoons wheat free soy sauce
>¼ teaspoon mustard powder
>½ teaspoon fresh ginger (or 1/8 teaspoon dried)
>2 tablespoons onion, chopped
>1 teaspoon garlic powder

1. In a small skillet or sauce pan, combine chicken broth, soy sauce, mustard, and ginger. Heat on medium heat, stirring, until spices dissolve.
2. If chicken is very cold or partially frozen, cut the chicken into strips. Add the chicken and chopped onion to the broth. Cook for 5-10 minutes on medium heat, until chicken is tender. Deglaze pan with water as needed.
3. Measure 4 ounces of cooked chicken onto each plate. Deglaze the drippings in the pan with water. Reduce liquid in pan to a thick sauce, stirring constantly. Pour sauce over chicken.

To make a complete meal of this, steam ¾ pound of broccoli or cauliflower and serve it topped with a tablespoon of butter, a little salt and pepper. I like the sauce over my vegetables, my husband prefers adding lemon juice to his.

Tangy Vinegar Chicken
Serves: 2
Exchanges: 1 protein

>¾ pound of chicken breast
>½ cup chicken broth
>½ cup apple cider vinegar
>¼ cup lemon juice
>2 tablespoons onion, chopped
>1 teaspoon garlic, minced (2 cloves)
>salt and pepper to taste

1. In a small skillet or sauce pan, combine chicken broth, vinegar, and lemon juice. Add onion, garlic, and chicken breast.
2. Cook thoroughly, approximately 5 – 10 minutes on medium heat. Add salt and pepper to taste. If necessary, deglaze pan with water to create sauce.

I love this as a make-ahead meal using strips of chicken, which I can layer onto a salad for a cold dinner when I'm out, such as when I'm attending a conference and know I need to eat before the final sessions of the day. To make a complete home meal of this, steam ¾ pound of broccoli or green beans and serve it topped with a tablespoon of butter, a little salt and pepper. Try a sprinkle of dill weed over your side vegetables.

Roasted Herbed Chicken

Serves: 2
Exchanges: 1 protein

> olive oil mister or cooking spray
> 2 chicken breast fillets (approximately ¾ pound)
> ½ teaspoon dried dill weed
> ½ teaspoon marjoram
> salt to taste

1. Preheat oven to 375°.
2. Spray a shallow baking dish with cooking spray.
3. Salt the chicken to taste. Spray the chicken with an olive oil mist or cooking spray. Alternating between the dill and marjoram, take a pinch of the herb and crush it between your fingers over the chicken, until you have created an herb crust. (You don't have to use all of the dill and marjoram if you prefer a lighter crust. I don't like any of the underlying chicken to show through.)
4. Place the chicken in the baking dish. Bake at 375° for one hour, or until the juices run clear.
5. Weigh out 4 ounces of cooked chicken for each portion.

*This is about as basic as chicken gets, but it's so delicious! Use the time while it's cooking to make your dinner salad and a more involved side vegetable, such as **Zucchini and Tomato Sauté**.*

Chicken Curry with Celery
Serves: 1
Exchanges: 1 protein, optional 1 vegetable

> 6 oz raw chicken, cubed
> ½ cup chicken broth
> ½ teaspoon curry powder
> 1/8 teaspoon turmeric
> ¼ teaspoon garlic powder
> ¼ teaspoon onion powder
> 2 tablespoons onion, minced
> salt and pepper to taste
> ¾ cup celery, chopped (6 oz) (optional)

1. In a small sauce pan, heat chicken broth over medium heat. Dissolve spices in chicken broth. Add chicken and onion. If using, add chopped celery.
2. Sauté until liquid reduces by half and chicken is fully cooked, approximately 5 – 10 minutes.

While this makes a nice hot dish, it's great for a picnic or pot luck as a cold chicken salad. Just multiply the chicken and celery by the number of people you'll be serving. Each serving will weigh approximately 8 ounces.

Roast Salmon and Broccoli
Serves: 2
Exchanges: 1 protein, 1 vegetable, 1 oil

> 12 oz broccoli florets
> ¼ cup onion, sliced
> 3 tablespoons olive oil
> ½ pound salmon fillet
> ¾ teaspoon salt, divided
> ½ teaspoon pepper, divided
> ¼ cup mayonnaise
> 1 tablespoon lemon juice
> ¼ teaspoon minced garlic

1. Heat oven to 450°. Line a rimmed baking sheet with parchment paper.
2. In a large bowl, toss together broccoli, onions, oil, ½ teaspoon salt, and ¼ teaspoon pepper until well coated. Spread in a single layer on the baking sheet. Roast for 15 minutes.
3. Season salmon with ¼ teaspoon salt and ¼ teaspoon pepper. Cut into 4 ounce servings. When vegetables are done roasting, make room on the baking sheet among the vegetables for the salmon slices. Make sure that the salmon is on the parchment paper, not vegetables, and that the vegetables are still in a single layer. Return to oven and roast for an additional 8 – 10 minutes.
4. Meanwhile, in a small bowl, combine mayonnaise, lemon juice, and garlic. Serve this sauce beside the fish – primarily for those who are not on the eating plan. Use sparingly, or count it as another serving of oil.

This is a very flexible recipe. I made it for my father's birthday, and he does not eat onions or garlic. I tossed the broccoli with the oil, salt, and pepper, then put his portion on the baking sheet, before tossing the onions with the remaining broccoli. Similarly, I mixed the mayonnaise and lemon juice first, removed his portion, and then added garlic to what remained. Onions or not, garlic or not, everyone loved it!

Poached Catfish
Serves: 2
Exchanges: 1 protein

> 8 oz catfish or other white fish (e.g. tilapia), divided
> 1 cup chicken broth
> 2 tablespoons lemon juice
> 2 tablespoons onion, chopped
> 1 teaspoon garlic, minced
> 1 teaspoon fresh ginger, minced (or ¼ teaspoon dried ginger)
> 1/8 teaspoon orange zest
> salt and pepper to taste

1. Divide the fish into 4 ounce servings. Season with salt and pepper to taste.
2. In a small frying pan, heat the broth over medium. Add lemon juice, onion, garlic, ginger, and orange zest.
3. Add fish and poach 5 – 10 minutes, until tender and cooked thoroughly.
4. Transfer fish to plates and top with remaining sauce.

I'm not a big white fish fan, but they're supposed to be healthier for you than the bigger fish like salmon or tuna. Apparently, they don't store as much mercury and other heavy metals in their bodies. Catfish is one of the few types of white fish I've found to actually have flavor, and I can buy it at my local Target.

Asiago Asparagus

Serves: 2
Exchanges: 1 protein, 1 vegetable

    1 pound asparagus stalks
    1 teaspoon garlic, minced
    4 oz sliced asiago cheese

1. Preheat oven to 350°. Line a baking sheet with parchment paper.
2. Trim asparagus to remove woody ends. (If both people are on the eating plan, start weighing as you get to the last few stalks, to ensure you have exactly 12 ounces of good asparagus.)
3. Place asparagus side-by-side on the parchment paper, in groups of 6 ounces.
4. Sprinkle with garlic. Top each group of asparagus with 2 ounces of asiago cheese slices.
5. Bake for 10 minutes.

This is my favorite light dinner, perfect for those nights when we have a meeting in the evening and want something light when we get home, that will be ready quickly. If you're on maintenance, pair it with a side of boiled quinoa for your grain exchange, since that cooks just as quickly.

Celery Lentil Soup
Serves: 4
Exchanges: 1 protein, 1 vegetable

    7.5 oz dried lentils or split peas
    2 tablespoons olive oil
    8 oz celery stalks, including tops and leaves, chopped
    16 oz tomatoes, chopped
    2 teaspoons dried marjoram
    1 tablespoon salt
    1 teaspoon dill seed

1. In a large pot, combine dried lentils or split peas and 2 ½ cups of water. Bring to a boil. Remove from heat and allow to soak for 1 hour. Drain and rinse.
2. In a Dutch Oven, heat oil and sauté celery until soft.
3. Add all other ingredients, including drained lentils or split peas. Add 6 cups of water. Bring to a boil. Cover, reduce heat, and simmer for 20 minutes.

This is a very flexible recipe. As long as the total vegetable weight is 24 ounces, you can include carrots, bell peppers, zucchini, cabbage, or anything else that you need to get out of your refrigerator. If you forget to presoak the lentils or split peas, you can start the recipe from step 2 – they'll just be a little chewy.

Vegetarian Chili

Serves: 4
Exchanges: 1 vegetable, 1 protein, 1 optional fat

- 2 tablespoons olive oil
- 3 carrots, thinly sliced
- 3 ribs celery, thinly sliced
- 1 large green bell pepper, diced
- 1 large yellow onion, chopped
- 3 – 5 cloves garlic, crushed
- 1 can (14 – 16 oz) diced tomatoes (or 1 ½ pounds fresh)
- 2 cans (14 – 16 oz) kidney beans, rinsed and drained (or 4 cups cooked)
- 1 can (6 oz) tomato paste
- 1 cup vegetable broth or water
- 2 tablespoons chili powder
- ½ teaspoon salt
- 1/8 teaspoon cinnamon
- ½ cup chopped olives as garnish (optional)

1. Heat the oil in a Dutch Oven over medium-high heat. Add the carrots, celery, bell pepper, and onion. Saute for 10 minutes, or until vegetables are soft.
2. Add the garlic and cook for an additional minute.
3. Stir in the tomatoes, beans, tomato paste, broth or water (use it to rinse out the tomato paste can), chili powder, salt, and cinnamon.
4. Cook for 45 – 60 minutes, stirring occasionally and adding water to keep from burning.
5. Ladle 10 ounce servings (6 ounces of beans and 4 ounces of cooked vegetable) into bowls. Garnish with chopped olives if desired.

Although this takes a while to cook, it requires very little effort after the initial slicing and dicing of vegetables. It's a great weekend dinner. You could probably also make it in a slow cooker, prepping through step 3 in the morning and cooking it on low all day, although I've never done that.

Casablanca Eggplant

Serves: 4
Exchanges: 1 vegetable, 1 oil, optional 1 grain

    4 oz quinoa (optional)
    1 large eggplant (1 ¼ - 1 ½ pounds)
    1 ½ teaspoon salt, divided
    3 tablespoons + 1 teaspoon olive oil
    1 medium summer squash or zucchini
    1 red (or orange or yellow) bell pepper
    3 medium tomatoes
    1 teaspoon garlic, minced (or 2 cloves, crushed)
    1 ¼ teaspoon ground cinnamon
    ¼ teaspoon ground pepper

1. Cut the eggplant into quarter-inch cubes. Place on a large baking sheet and sprinkle with 1 teaspoon salt. Let stand for 30 minutes.
2. Meanwhile, if using the quinoa, boil 2 cups of water with a dash of salt. Add the quinoa, cover, and simmer for 12 minutes or until the water is absorbed. Take off the heat, fluff, and let stand for 15 minutes.
3. Cut squash or zucchini into quarter-inch cubes. Dice the pepper and tomatoes.
4. Heat 3 tablespoons of oil in a large skillet or wok over medium-high heat. Rinse and drain eggplant. Add eggplant, squash, and pepper to oil. Cook, stirring, 8 – 10 minutes or until vegetables are soft. Transfer vegetable mixture to a large bowl.
5. Add remaining teaspoon of oil to pan. Add tomatoes, garlic, cinnamon, remaining ½ teaspoon salt, and pepper. Cook, stirring, 3 – 5 minutes or until tomatoes begin to break down.
6. Add tomato mixture to bowl containing eggplant mixture, and stir to combine. Allow to cool to room temperature.
7. Serve 4 ounces of vegetable mixture as a stand-alone dish or serve over each serving of quinoa.

Because this dish is both complex and flavorful, I usually pair it with a simple protein, such as a cheese plate or Greek yogurt. This is more time- and labor-intensive than most of my recipes, but it can be made in advance, making it perfect for pot-lucks or entertaining. If you're really pressed for time, you can skip the step for sweating the eggplant, add it to the oil before the other vegetables, and cook off the extra liquid.

Zucchini Tomato Sauté
Serves: 2
Exchanges: 1 vegetable, 1 oil, optional 1 grain

- 2 oz dry quinoa or millet (optional)
- 2 large zucchini
- 2 medium tomatoes
- ½ teaspoon salt
- 3 tablespoons olive oil

1. If using, boil the quinoa or millet according to package directions.
2. Slice the zucchini wafer thin with a mandoline. Chop the tomatoes.
3. Heat the oil in a wok or large skillet. Add sliced zucchini. Sauté until the zucchini is completely limp.
4. Add tomatoes. Cook, stirring continuously, until tomatoes are hot. Stir in salt.
5. Serve 4 ounces of zucchini mixture as a stand-alone side dish, or over optional quinoa or millet.

This is a great dish for company. Simply increase the amount of quinoa, zucchini, tomato, and salt for the number of people you're serving. Add one additional tablespoon of oil per additional person. You really need a mandoline to make this dish properly, unless your knife skills are much better than mine. I'm not a fan of the taste of zucchini, but the thin slices practically dissolve, making the taste of the tomatoes primary.

Roasted Broccoli and Onion
Serves: 2
Exchanges: 1 vegetable, 1 oil

>   12 oz broccoli florets
>   ¼ cup onion, sliced
>   3 tablespoons olive oil
>   ½ teaspoon salt
>   ¼ teaspoon pepper, divided

1. Heat oven to 450°. Line a rimmed baking sheet with parchment paper.
2. In a large bowl, toss together broccoli, onions, oil, salt, and pepper until well coated. Spread in a single layer on the baking sheet. Roast for 23 – 25 minutes.

*Yes, this is just the vegetable part of the **Salmon and Broccoli** dinner. My husband liked it so much that he asked if we could have our broccoli this way from now on instead of steamed, so this is now a standard side dish in our household. You can substitute other vegetables for the broccoli, such as cauliflower, carrots, sweet potatoes, potatoes, and green beans.*

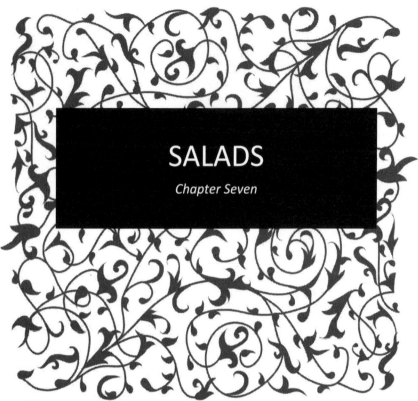

SALADS
Chapter Seven

Growing up, I thought there were two things called "salad". One was a pile of anemic, bitter lettuce, sometimes with a few dried out carrot slivers on top for color, that I choked down as quickly as I could. The other salad was protein or fruit of some kind, mixed with Jell-O and/or mayonnaise. These were served when we had guests, because they looked very pretty. The taste was irrelevant.

The nightly dinner salads that are part of the Bright Line Eating program have little to nothing in common with either of those sad excuses for salad. Instead, they are creative extravaganzas that are a feast for both the eyes and the taste buds.

I find this is one of the natural pressure release valves of the eating plan. Since you write a list of what you're going to eat the night before, you lose some flexibility when it comes to adapting to your situation. Running late? No chance to change your designated dinner plans – but you can get a salad on the table quickly, then start cooking the rest of your meal without going crazy from hunger.

It also allows you to try new foods that you found at the grocery store or farmers' market without needing to create an eating-plan-compliant entrée featuring whatever it is you bought. I find virtually any vegetable can be added to a salad either raw, or steamed for 5 – 10 minutes then cooled.

You can get as crazy as you want with inspiration. I made a "Florida Gators" salad in honor of my brother's alma mater that consisted entirely of green and orange foods, served in bright blue bowls.

To start, decide on your base of greens. The most common greens are:

- romaine lettuce ("Caesar" blend, leaf, or head)
- mixed iceberg lettuce and cabbage ("American" blend)
- spring greens
- spinach leaves
- 50/50 blend of spring greens and spinach leaves

These are sold in large plastic bags or bins year round at the grocery store. You can also get gourmet heads of lettuce in season from the farmers' market in more unusual varieties such as Boston, Bibb, or Butterhead.

Experiment with the different types to see which flavors you and your family prefer. My husband likes spring greens and I like spinach leaves, so I usually use the 50/50 blend for our dinner salads. If the only 50/50 blends in stock at the store are close to their sell-buy date, I'll buy a fresher package of one of the other varieties so that the greens don't turn black and bitter. Sometimes, just to be different, I'll grab a head of Napa cabbage to use as a base.

Then decide what your primary layers of the salad will be. My most common layers are shredded carrots, chopped heritage tomatoes, sliced cucumbers, and chopped bell peppers in red, yellow, or orange. Prepare your layers in advance, because when it comes time to assemble your salad, you'll be working against the clock for the timer on your digital scale. Don't worry about cutting up too much. You can always put whatever you don't use one night into plastic baggies to save for the next night's salad.

This is also where you can add interesting vegetables from the farmers' market, or finish off whatever vegetable you were serving as part of the main dish the night before. (For example, if you buy heads of broccoli, you'll end up with some extra florets after you weigh out 12 ounces.)

Finally, decide on your garnish. My husband loves raw pumpkin seeds on the top of his salads. I'm a huge fan of baked parmesan crisps (a fantastic crouton alternative). Keep in mind that the garnish must be applied with a light hand, or else it will cost you one of your fat servings. I find 0.1 – 0.3 ounces is a good amount of garnish.

When assembling salads, it's easiest to weigh the first salad bowl, zero out the scale, add 2 – 3 ounces of greens, then repeat the process for all of the other bowls, ensuring that they all start with the same base weight of greens. (Even if you use identical bowls from the same set, the weight may read slightly differently depending on where you put the bowl on the scale, so always start from a zero reading.)

Complete each salad individually by putting the bowl on the scale, zeroing out the scale, and adding enough of your layers to bring you to a total weight of approximately 7.8 ounces. Then add your garnish to take you to an even 8 ounces.

For example, your salad may look like:

- 2 ounces of romaine lettuce
- 1 ounce of shredded carrot
- 1.7 ounces of chopped bell peppers
- 1.8 ounces of chopped heritage tomatoes
- 1.3 ounces of sliced cucumber
- 0.2 ounces of baked parmesan crisps

You'd start by zeroing out the scale and adding 2 ounces of romaine. Repeat for every bowl. Put the first bowl back on the scale and zero it out. Add carrot, peppers, tomatoes, and cucumber until the scale reads 5.8 ounces. Top with .2 ounces of crisps. The scale will read 6.0 ounces. That, plus your initial 2 ounces of lettuce make up your 8 ounce salad.

You may be wondering about salad dressing. My view is that salad dressing is a disguise for a bad salad. If you use a variety of fresh, ripe produce, there's no need to cover up the flavor. Also, it is very difficult to find salad dressings without added sweeteners. If you absolutely must have salad dressing, there are some Caesar dressings with no sweeteners, or you can use a classic mix of balsamic vinegar and olive oil.

SAMPLE MEAL PLANS
Chapter Eight

I f you have never created meal plans based on food exchanges before, you may still be a bit confused about how all of this comes together into something you can eat. With that in mind, I've offered a few sample meal plans for specific types of days.

The four sample days are: Old Faithful, my standard menu when I don't have anything special to do that day; Lunch on the Run, when I need something I can carry with me to eat somewhere and someplace without access to a kitchen or possibly even silverware; Evening Meeting, when I will have a meeting after work and will eat dinner afterwards; and Family Day, when I have more time to cook and want to provide a special dining experience.

Old Faithful

Breakfast	**Lemon Water** **Oatmeal and Banana** 2 Eggs Over Easy
Lunch	Water **Turkey Salad** 1 Apple 25 Pistachios
Dinner	Water 8 oz Dinner Salad **Sweet Mustard Chicken** Steamed Green Beans with 1 Tablespoon of Butter

Lunch on the Run

Breakfast	**Lemon Water** **Oatmeal and Banana** 2 Soft Boiled Eggs
Lunch	Bottled Water 6 oz Carrot and Celery Sticks 2 oz Cheese Slices on 1 Apple, Sliced 25 Pistachios
Dinner	Water 8 oz Dinner Salad **Salmon and Broccoli**

Evening Meeting

Breakfast	**Lemon Water**
	Berry Good Oatmeal
	4 oz cottage cheese
Lunch	LaCroix Sparkling Water
	Simple Tuna Nicoise Salad with
	2 oz Avocado
	2 Kiwis
Dinner	Water
	8 oz Dinner Salad
	Asiago Asparagus
	25 Pistachios

Note: I carry the pistachios to the meeting in my purse "just in case" because I get nervous about low blood sugar.

Family Day

Breakfast	**Lemon Water**
	Gruyere Egg
	Breakfast Potatoes
Lunch	Iced Tea
	Burger with Salsa
	6 oz Watermelon
	½ oz Sunflower Seeds
Dinner	Water
	8 oz Dinner Salad
	Vegetarian Chili with
	2 oz olives

FINAL THOUGHTS
Chapter Nine

That is everything you need to know, to be able to create healthy meals like I did. Hopefully, if you are diabetic or pre-diabetic, you will also find your A1C levels dropping – along with improving your liver function and losing weight.

I would love it if the diabetes epidemic could be reversed simply by getting everyone to eat clean, with no sugars or processed grains, even if they don't feel the need to do the complete Bright Line Eating program.

If you also have a personal story to share, or a collection of favorite recipes you'd like to make into a cookbook, you can learn how to write and publish a book in 3 months or less by going to: http://bit.ly/2vy5SYk

Made in the USA
Monee, IL
30 December 2019